WEST CHICAGO PUBLIC LIBRARY DISTRICT
3 6653 00190 8809

P9-CML-091

Amazing Animals

Kangaroos

Anna Rebus

WEIGL PUBLISHERS INC.

Published by Weigl Publishers Inc.
350 5th Avenue, Suite 3304
New York, NY USA 10118-0069

Library of Congress Cataloging-in-Publication Data

Rebus, Anna.
Kangaroos / Anna Rebus.
p. cm. – (Amazing animals)
Includes index.
ISBN 1-59036-393-0 (hard cover : alk. paper)
– ISBN 1-59036-399-X (soft cover : alk. paper)
1. Kangaroos–Juvenile literature. I. Title. II. Amazing animals series.
QL737.M35R43 2006
599.2'22–dc22

2005027352

Printed in the United States of America
2 3 4 5 6 7 8 9 0 12 11 10 09 08

COVER: Kangaroos continuously grow throughout their lives.

Editor
Heather C. Hudak
Design and Layout
Terry Paulhus

About This Book

This book tells you all about kangaroos. Find out where they live and what they eat. Discover how people are working hard to protect kangaroos. You can also read about kangaroo myths and legends from Australia.

Words in **bold** are explained in the Words to Know section at the back of the book.

Useful Websites

Addresses in this book take you to the home pages of websites that have information about kangaroos.

All of the Internet URLs given in the book were valid at the time of publication. However, due to the dynamic nature of the Internet, some addresses may have changed, or sites may have ceased to exist since publication. While the author and publisher regret any inconvenience this may cause readers, no responsibility for any such changes can be accepted by either the author or the publisher.

Contents

Pages 4—5
Meet the Kangaroo

Pages 6—7
A Very Special Animal

Pages 8—9
How Kangaroos Hop

Pages 10—11
How Kangaroos Eat

Pages 12—13
Where Kangaroos Live

Pages 14—15
Friends and Enemies

Pages 16—17
Growing Up

Pages 18—19
Under Threat

Pages 20—21
Myths and Legends

Pages 22—23
Quiz/Find out More

Page 24
Words to Know/Index

Meet the Kangaroo

Kangaroos are remarkable animals. They live in Australia, New Guinea, and some nearby islands. Kangaroos are a type of **marsupial**. A newborn kangaroo grows inside a pouch on the outside of its mother's belly.

Kangaroos are the only large animals that move by hopping. Female kangaroos are called flyers. Male kangaroos are called boomers.

▶ About 50 million kangaroos live in Australia.

The Kangaroo Family

There are more than 50 types of kangaroos.

- gray kangaroos
- rat kangaroos
- red kangaroos
- tree kangaroos
- wallabies
- wallaroos

▲ The kangaroo population does well when there is a steady source of water.

A Very Special Animal

A kangaroo's body is made for hopping and bouncing. Kangaroos hop a long way to find food and to escape enemies. They also have a very long tail that helps them stay balanced while hopping.

A kangaroo has four legs. The front two legs are short, and the paws look like human hands. Kangaroos have large back legs and big feet. Kangaroos are called macropods, *macro* meaning "large" and *pod* meaning "foot."

▶ Red kangaroos use their small front legs for grooming and eating.

Useful Websites

www.australianfauna.com

Search kangaroos in the alphabetical listing to learn more about how they hop.

Kangaroo fur can be many different colors.

A kangaroo can move each ear separately to listen for danger.

Only female kangaroos have a pouch.

Kangaroos have small front paws.

The long tail helps a kangaroo to stay balanced while hopping.

Kangaroos have powerful hind legs.

How Kangaroos Hop

All kangaroos move around by hopping. They have three short toes and one long middle toe. A kangaroo's legs have strong muscles and **tendons** that act like springs. These features allow a kangaroo to leap forward a great distance in a single hop. Kangaroos are perfectly designed to hop.

▼ Kangaroo feet can measure up to 1.5 feet (0.5 meters) long.

The Amazing Kangaroo

- A large kangaroo can hop at a speed of 20 miles per hour (32 kilometers per hour).
- A large male red kangaroo can weigh as much as 200 pounds (90 kilograms).
- The yellow-footed rock-wallaby can cover 16 feet (5 m) in one leap.
- Kangaroos are excellent swimmers.

▲ Gray kangaroos can leap more than 30 feet (9 m) in one jump, and can reach heights of 10 feet (3 m).

How Kangaroos Eat

Kangaroos are **herbivores**. Baby kangaroos drink their mother's milk until they are old enough to eat plants.

Bettongs and potoroos are part of the kangaroo family. They like to eat worms, insects, and fungus that they dig up.

Kangaroos are nocturnal, meaning they are more active at night. They prefer to eat at night when it is cool.

▶ Kangaroos eat green plants that are high in protein.

Terrific Teeth

- Kangaroo teeth are made for eating plants.
- Kangaroos have large molars that help grind up tough plant material.
- A kangaroo's molar teeth can be replaced up to 16 times in a lifetime.

▼ Kangaroos are 30 percent smaller than they were 40,000 years ago.

Where Kangaroos Live

Kangaroos live in forests, on open plains, and on rocky hills. They have also been seen near swamps and even in the rain forest.

Kangaroos live near shrubs and bushes because these plants help them hide from **predators**. Rock-wallabies like to live where they can hop over rocks and boulders. Tree kangaroos are found in trees and live alone.

▼ Brush-tailed bettongs are only active at night.

Useful Websites

www.nc-claws.org/bettongs.htm

Search bettongs at this website to learn more about their daily activities.

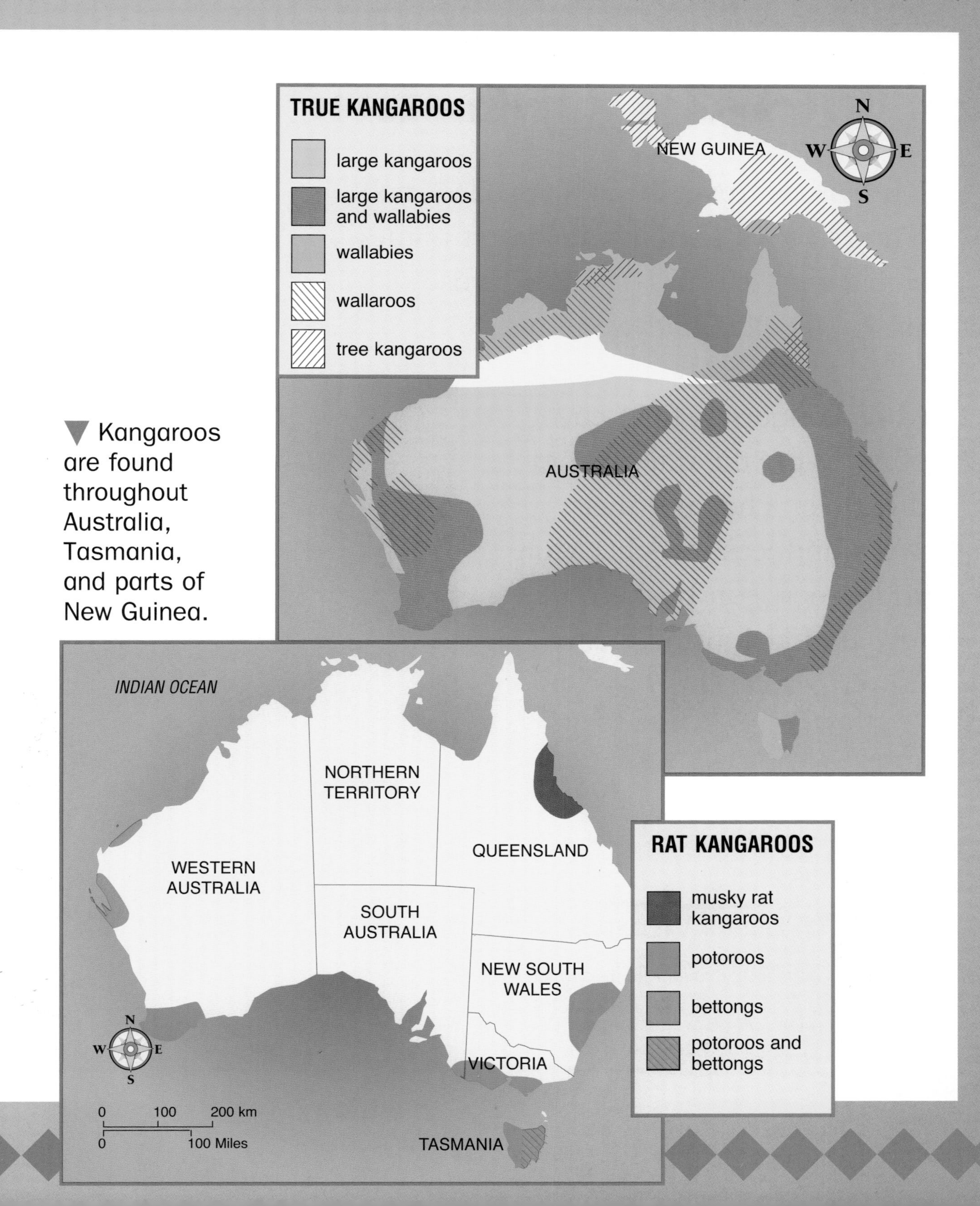

▼ Kangaroos are found throughout Australia, Tasmania, and parts of New Guinea.

Friends and Enemies

Kangaroos travel in groups called **mobs**. They share their forest or desert homes with many animals, such as birds, snakes, koalas, and wombats.

▼ Male kangaroos use their front paws to knock each other off balance.

Male kangaroos fight each other to get the attention of a female. They use their paws and legs to fight. Male kangaroos lean back on their tails and kick using their powerful hind legs.

Useful Websites

www.australianwildlife.com.au

Click on kangaroos at this website to learn more about their behavior.

Kangaroo Companions

Kangaroos share the forest and desert with many other animals.

- bandicoots
- birds
- **dingoes**
- frogs
- koalas
- lizards
- possums
- snakes
- wombats

▲ Kangaroos travel in groups, but individual members move at will.

Growing Up

A mother kangaroo gives birth to a baby kangaroo called a joey. The joey is the size of a bumblebee and is not fully formed.

The joey will spend more than 120 days suckling milk in its mother's pouch. In the pouch, the joey begins to grow.

When the joey is old enough, it will leave its mother's pouch for short periods of time. If the joey senses danger, it will dive into its mother's pouch headfirst.

▶ A joey weighs less than 0.04 ounces (1 gram) and measures 1 inch (2 centimeters) long when it is born.

▶ In some species of kangaroos, daughters stay close to their mothers, even after they give birth to their own joeys.

Growth Chart

30 days	0.35 ounces (1 g)	The tiny joey leaves the birth canal and crawls up to its mother's pouch.
120-130 days	2.2 pounds (1 kg)	The joey's body is pink and hairless, and its eyes are still closed.
190 days	4.5 pounds (2 kg)	The joey comes out of the pouch for the first time. Fur starts to grow.
7-10 months	8.5 to 11 pounds (4 to 5 kg)	The joey leaves its mother's pouch completely.

Under Threat

Today, some types of kangaroos are in danger of dying out. Many people are working hard to save them from **extinction**.

Humans are the biggest threat to kangaroos. Each year, thousands of kangaroos are hit by cars on the road. People also hunt kangaroos for food, fur, and sport.

▼ The Australian government has laws to protect kangaroos.

Useful Websites

www.kidsplanet.org/factsheets/kangaroos.html

Learn more about kangaroos by visiting this website.

What Do You Think?

In some areas of Australia, there are too many kangaroos, and they are considered pests. They compete with cattle and sheep for grasses to eat and water to drink. Should people be allowed to kill kangaroos to ensure cattle and sheep have enough to eat and drink?

▲ Most kangaroos are active at dawn and dusk. Natural light is low at these times, making it difficult to see kangaroos on the side of the road.

Myths and Legends

For thousands of years, **Aboriginal Australians** have told stories about kangaroos.

The First Kangaroos

One day a group of men were out hunting. They were suddenly hit by a very powerful windstorm. They found a cave and waited for the storm to pass. The hunters saw strange animals being carried by the wind across the sky.

The men had never seen animals like these before. They soon realized that the wind had brought in these animals from a distant land. The animals began stretching out their hind legs and tails to reach solid ground. Some of the animals finally made it to the ground.

▲ The name kangaroo likely comes from the Aboriginal Australian word *gangurru*, which means kangaroo.

The hunters noticed that the animals had stretched so hard that their tails and hind legs had become very long. The animals began eating the grass and drinking the water. It was just the sort of place the animals liked, and they wanted to stay.

▼ Kangaroos have been a source of clothing and food for Aboriginal Australians for thousands of years.

Today, these animals are called kangaroos.

Kangaroo Art

Aboriginal Australians have painted pictures of kangaroos on rock and bark for thousands of years.

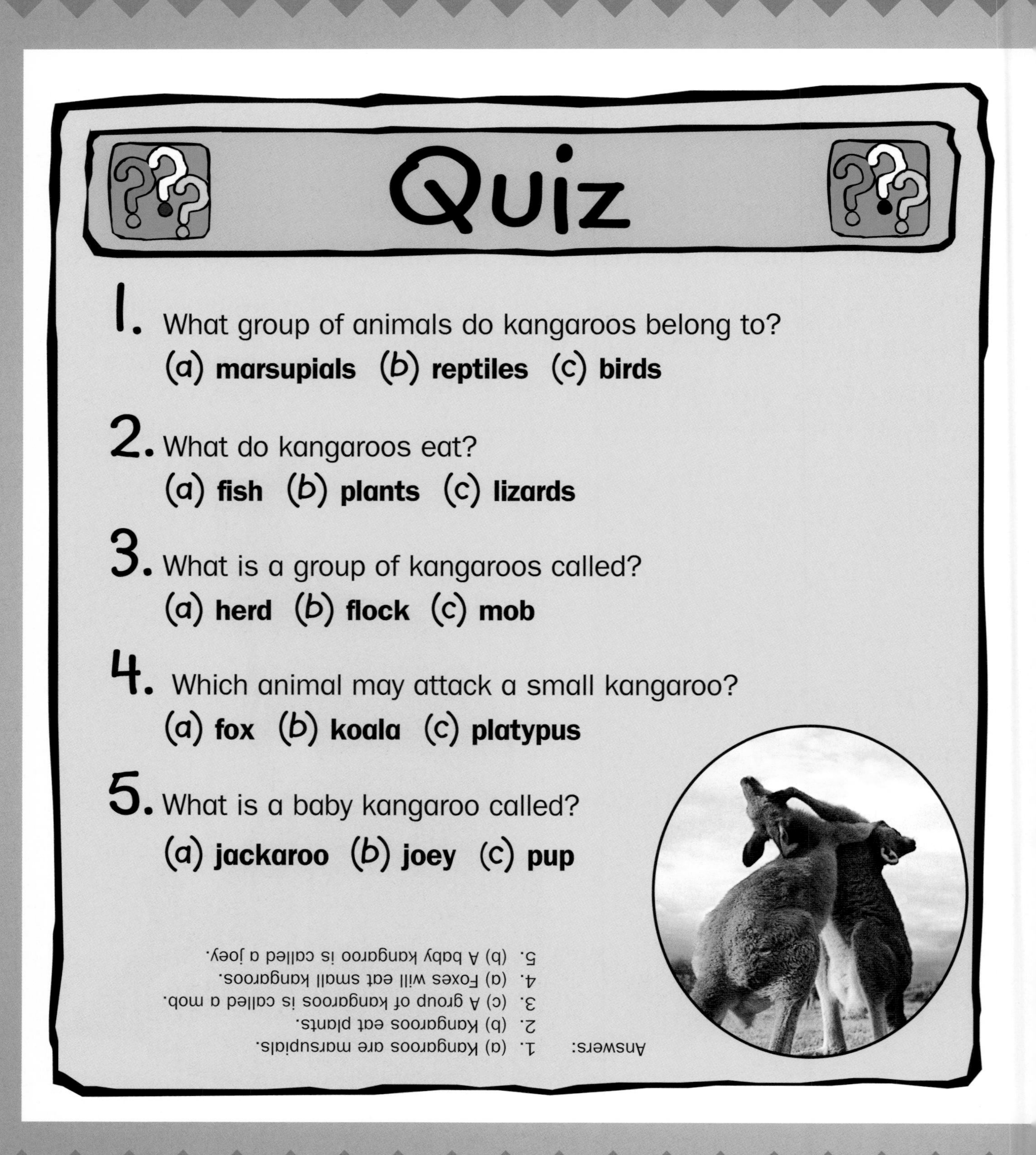

Quiz

1. What group of animals do kangaroos belong to?
   (a) **marsupials** (b) **reptiles** (c) **birds**

2. What do kangaroos eat?
   (a) **fish** (b) **plants** (c) **lizards**

3. What is a group of kangaroos called?
   (a) **herd** (b) **flock** (c) **mob**

4. Which animal may attack a small kangaroo?
   (a) **fox** (b) **koala** (c) **platypus**

5. What is a baby kangaroo called?
   (a) **jackaroo** (b) **joey** (c) **pup**

Answers:
1. (a) Kangaroos are marsupials.
2. (b) Kangaroos eat plants.
3. (c) A group of kangaroos is called a mob.
4. (a) Foxes will eat small kangaroos.
5. (b) A baby kangaroo is called a joey.

Find out More

To find out more about kangaroos, visit the websites in this book. You can also write to these organizations.

National Wildlife Federation
11100 Wildlife Center Drive
Reston, VA 20190-5362

World Wildlife Fund U.S.
1250 24th Street NW
Washington, DC 20037

World Wildlife Fund Canada
245 Eglinton Ave. East, Suite 410
Toronto, ON M4P 3J1
CANADA

Words to Know

Aboriginal Australians
descendents of original inhabitants

dingoes
Australian wild dogs

extinction
no longer living on Earth

herbivores
animals that eat plants

marsupial
a type of animal that gives birth to undeveloped young

mobs
groups of kangaroos that live together

predators
animals that hunt other animals for food

tendons
bands of tissue that connect muscles

Index

Aboriginal Australians 20, 21

birth 16
boomer 4

dingoes 15, 19

eating 6, 10, 11, 21
extinction 18

flyer 4

hop 4, 6, 7, 8, 9, 12

joey 16, 17

macropod 6
marsupial 4
mobs 14

pouch 4, 7, 16, 17

size 16, 17

teeth 11